Pandemic Birthdays are the ~~Worst~~ Best!

A Humorous Gift of Verse for People Celebrating Birthdays Under Quarantine

ISBN: 9798649385626

BIRTHDAY GIFT SERIES

Good Gift Books

Note from the Author

This year has been challenging, to say the least. It's clear that the world is facing enormous issues, and in light of the "big" issues, having your birthday in the middle of a pandemic is admittedly a smaller concern. But it's still an unpleasant experience if we are all being honest.

The ability to celebrate our birthdays whenever and however we want isn't something we've ever viewed as a privilege, but now we know better. We may have taken situations like this for granted in the past, but something tells me we won't for many years to come. So, in light of all those people out there celebrating via video chat, I decided to pen this verse that puts a positive spin on a pandemic birthday, highlighting its uniqueness as opposed to its unpleasantness.

What I say is that we find a way to celebrate this birthday in the most unique, and perhaps weirdest ways, we can think of. This not only will make this birthday special, but also create a beautiful memory of the birthday we celebrated under quarantine. Besides, we might just be remembering birthdays during normal years a little more pleasantly than they deserve.

Best wishes and Happy Birthday!

— *Violet Jade*

There's one thing that you must admit ...

This is a birthday you'll never forget.

The odds are good that you'll never get ...

A birthday party that's this "no sweat."

At the moment it's hard to think straight ...

About how birthday parties aren't that great.

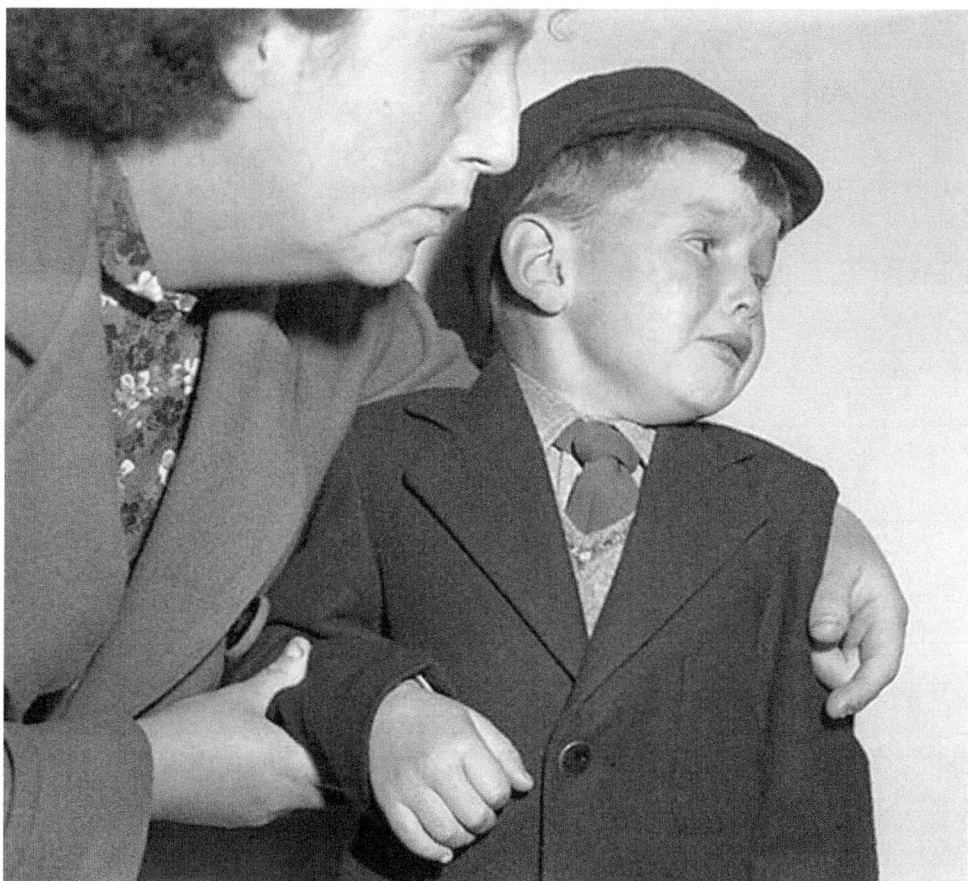

There are things about them that we hate;

Things you won't have this year, I'll demonstrate:

During normal years you're forced to go along,

With the person who
feels the need to
belt the song ...

The person who asks,
"how old are you?"
all night long ...

The person whose
social distance was
always wrong ...

The person who you know is there just to get cake ...

The person who talks and talks, never takes a break ...

The person whose personality is rather fake ...

The person whose, um,
er, uh, name I think is
"Jake" ...

The person who won't
stop saying that you're
getting old ...

The person who, despite their hand, just refuses to fold ...

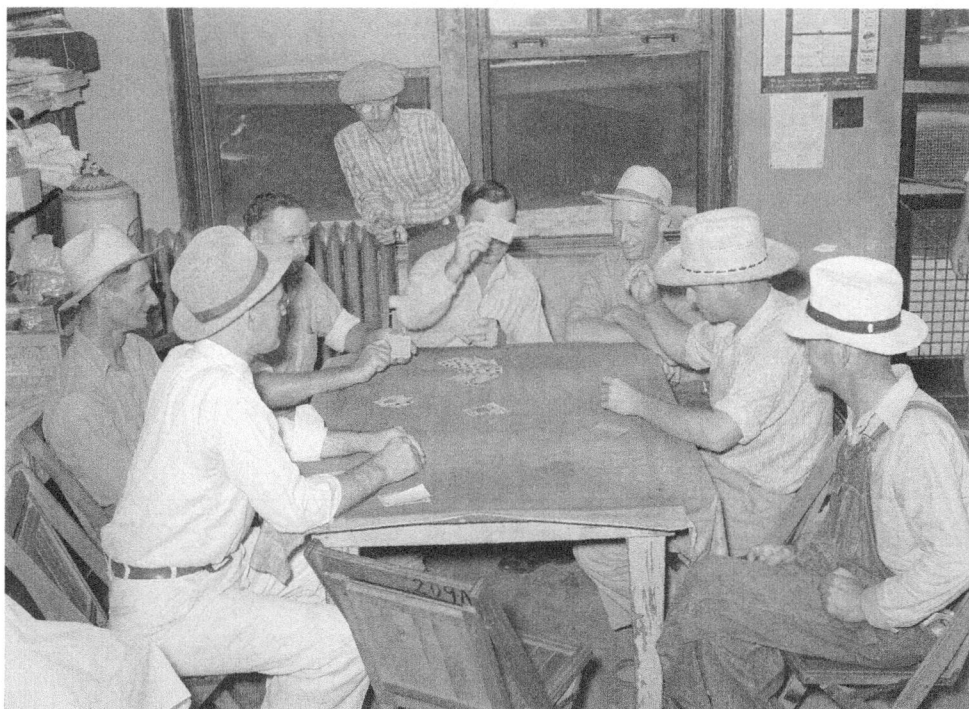

The person who thinks
their story is the
greatest ever told ...

The person whose breath smells like a bucket of mold ...

The person who talks
about all the people
they know ...

The person who can't stop saying: you must see this show ...

The person who wants to be in charge of the stereo ...

The person,
when the party's over,
never will go ...

These people on birthdays are just the worst ...

It's a day where you're supposed to be first.

Causing your lips to permanently be pursed ...

And there are also ways you are often coerced:

To eat so much sugar, it's simply insane ...

To put out fires, which
we could just refrain ...

To put up with people who always complain ...

To care that the birthday song is public domain ...

During our lives, in this current existence ...

We shouldn't put up an
ounce of resistance ...

And just have some
fun while we socially
distance ...

But, oh, how I want
all this to stop this
instance ...

How much you
miss things like
shaking hands ...

Or being able to go hear some live bands ...

Or that loud cackle of laughter after a joke lands ...

Or not having to settle for the sub par t.p. brands ...

The fact of the matter
is we need to admit ...

We took too much for granted until we lost it.

But instead of letting our happiness take such a hit.

A better alternative, please allow me to submit:

I have an idea for what we could do ...

To keep this birthday special for you ...

You can give your dog a wacky hairdo ...

You can draw on your forehead a birthday tattoo ...

Birthday Boy

You can hop in your bathtub and pretend it's a canoe ...

Print some fake money and hide it in a show ...

You can sing to the
neighbors for your
Broadway debut ...

Start a fight with a kite and pretend that you lose ...

But something of value that you can't help but do ...

You can see the world from a new point of view ...

And on this birthday, it's presented to you ...

It's a chance for a birthday where your perspective GREW!

This is not a birthday to shed any tears ...

Or to reflect on how everything's grinding your gears ...

And so, to you, on this birthday, I give three cheers ...

A birthday you'll remember for all of your years!

Happy Birthday to all the Pandemic Birthday Folks!!!

We hope you've enjoyed your copy of
Pandemic Birthdays are the ~~Worst~~ Best!

GOOD GIFT
Books

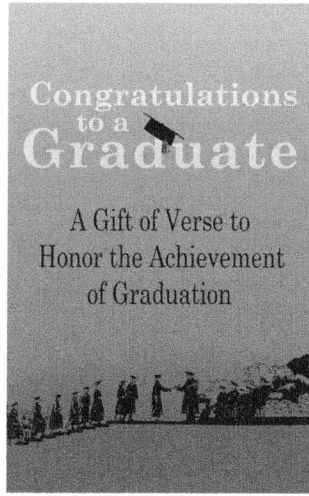

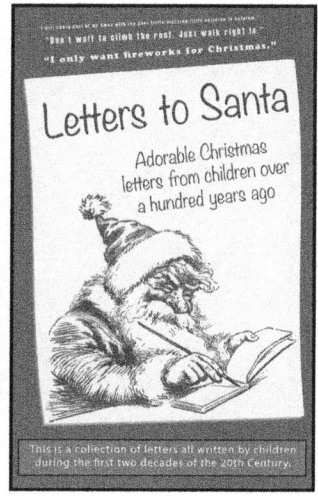

Made in the USA
Monee, IL
02 June 2020